DEDICATION

To the two fine souls that shaped my life: Nwokeke & Fide

CONTENTS

CHAPTER	PAGE

PREFACE

Men's ideas are the most direct emanations of their material state- Karl Marx

This book broaches questions on wealth creation, and interrogates many issues bordering on how it can be managed. Since the principles of economic science depict human behaviours, I have tried to corroborate my personal experience with my studies of human exploits in the economic world to motivate the general readers, especially the students of entrepreneurship.

I wanted to write a book that would capture the excitement of labour and thoughts in the past- the mistakes and the triumphs. So the book is an attempt to address the subject of entrepreneurship from historical and philosophical perspective, with the view of exploring the cult of interaction between an entrepreneur and wealth, and how it affects society. In a more strict sense, this aspect of studies is known as philosophy of entrepreneurship. The Wealth Manager is a departure from the economic theory that sees man essentially as a selfish being- all his motive is to make profit and his behaviours are governed by certain economic laws. While I can't refute the economic nature of man in its entirety, this book views man as a thinking and social being capable of making his own laws, or imbibing certain habits, of increasing his technical and social knowledge and of mastering his economic destiny.

Therefore, the soul of this work is the emphasis on the role of individual capacity in wealth management. Put differently, it shows that economic change- whether positive or negative, is always initiated by man, his ideas and actions. I have deeply been influenced by the spirit imbedded in the works of great thinkers like Plato, Sun Tzu, et al. But surprisingly, or rather, paradoxically, most of them were more of political thinkers. Yet it was the spirit that led me to consult classical and modern works on, and related to Economic thoughts.

Hence, I'm mostly indebted to Dr. B.A. Mojeutan, a retired Intellectual Historian at Ibadan School of History, who exposed me to my first knowledge of philosophical synthesis. I believe the knowledge has paid off, because most of the ideas formulated in my book are mine- they have been gleaned from many years of readership. I also remember that it was from this great tutor that I learnt the art of writing concisely. The last chapter of the book is an exhilarating mental exercise laden with lessons of human response to greatness. I want to specially thank my wife, Chidinma. She has reposed in me, an undying confidence even against all odds.

My focus on wealth is informed by the wealth of impoverishment in Africa. This however doesn't make it a book for Africans; it owes its form to the continent in which I grew up and participated in starting up business. Yet the book is a wakeup call for prospective entrepreneurs and those who are already in the business of managing wealth all over the world. Poverty does not have nationality, and it is both a curse and an obstacle to quality livelihood. You would not agree less with me if you put into consideration, the dehumanizing nature of poverty and the destructive temptations it subjects people to. It is pertinent to note as this book proves, that it is easy to write about wealth than acquiring it. Wealth requires not just productive labour but positive thoughts. Susan Taylor aptly submits that:

Thoughts have power; thoughts are energy. And you can make your world or break it by your own thinking.

The ability of man to tinker on how he can rise to fend for his wants and equally add value to society is the central theme of this book.

There are many books on wealth and this work has not been written to add to their numbers. This book is armed with a different approach. It has a historical undertone and apparently appears as philosophy of wealth acquisition. It also has some bearing on political economy. This is because it's hard to separate economics or monetary issues from politics. The emphasis is on human capacity not only to think but to think about the thought itself and survive in a society governed by man-made laws. To this end, the pages have been supported with relevant quotes, case histories and anecdotes. I hope the reader will be most indulgent to find enough places where critiques are needed to create rooms for more interrogations on the subject.

Chuka Okeke
Swift Current, SK
Canada
chukanwokeke@gmail.com

CHAPTER ONE

WEALTH ACQUISITION

"You are not wealthy until you have something money can't buy "- Garth Brooks

The nature of wealth is transitory. With determination and clear cut ideas of what we want to achieve, we can do everything possible to make the best out of life, to be fulfilled and find happiness. In the end, what we don't know is what we don't possess. If you are alive without the knowledge of the right contents, you would not know when you are dying or living in the economic sense of the word. Hence, the transitory nature of wealth means that by accident or process of attrition, it can disappear.

It follows that durability which we assume every fortune carries on its forehead is not actually an indispensable feature of wealth. The idea, as we shall see will help us to also understand the fleeting nature of wealth. But we can ascribe a place to durability in determining the amount of wealth in any material product. Let's say we have crude oil, we can measure how potentially wealthy we are by its quality which determine the value. Then, we will begin to ask questions as to how much of it is in our possession or how much labour we need to put in to produce the quantity that will take care of our wellbeing. But apart from satisfying the wants of man in abundance, wealth in its pure form must be useful and possessable. Wealth acquisition, therefore, is an economic process that creates certain social conditions which enable man to enjoy his wants.

In life, even when wealth phases out, one thing will not pass away. It is our knowledge of the physical and spiritual realms. In pursuit of material products, man and his economic ideas are not alone. He needs a belief system or the spirit world reasoning. He also needs to understand the tact in dealing with what I call the F factors, namely- friends, families and "fools". It entails the mastery and utilization of the environment. The reader will be surprised to read that asides ideas, family and friends, he also needs fools in pursuit of wealth. This is because wealth impresses family and friends, but confuses the fool. In any market, one business would struggle to make a "fool" out of others by taking advantage of their ignorance; ignorance which fails to innovate, and which fails to realize that someone else is using its blindness as a means to an end. We shall later see an example of how the fool factor evolves.

There are so many ways or methods to do business, but a religious use of proper methods yields better result without any intention to hurt either the environment or people; this defines the moral aspect of wealth acquisition. Each business chooses the method that allows it to compete favourably in the market. A society that condones human efforts that impede on equitable distribution of wealth does so at its own detriment. Monopoly is possible when other competitors lack certain business strategies to diversify the market or if the government allows it. A very close example was the "Trust" strategy adopted by Standard Oil, a company founded by John D. Rockefeller to vindicate his efforts to enjoy the dividends from oil business. At some point, the company gained a monopoly in the oil sector by controlling 90 % of the oil production in the US.

Other companies were disappointed and felt like "fools" because they realised they had been driven out of business. The implication was that Standard Oil Trust fixed whatever price it believed the market could afford. The essence of imbibing morality in business is to ensure that reliable goods and services are supplied, and to ensure that no one is hurt in the process. Rockefeller did argue that while he sold the oil products at cheaper rates, he never compromised the efficiency or quality of the products. But the whole idea of Trust didn't go down with the American society because they insisted on a fair playing ground for every business. It was not a surprise that Sherman Antitrust Act of 1890 proposed by Senator John Sherman was initiated in the Senate. It dragged on until the US Supreme Court in its 1911 rulings dissolved the Standard oil empire into different entities. Sherman anti-Trust act put an end to unrestrained competition and other practices geared towards unreasonable combination.

The court ruling gives us a legal perspective on wealth acquisition. It clearly shows that apart from natural resources and sophistication of physical technologies, laws and institutional factors play significant roles in wealth creation. These elements can be described as social technologies involved in wealth acquisition. Eric D. Beinhocker defined social technology as methods and designs for organizing people in pursuit of a goal or goals. It includes all the factors necessary for organizing. Managers have the rights to guard their businesses for themselves only if those rights are well defined and do not interfere with others, or serve their interest at the detriment of other managers; norms and laws, or public policies are determinant factors of how wealth is created. It is evident that those that make and interpret laws are instrumental in creating the condition that allows people to acquire wealth in an organized manner.

However, the governing principles of wealth acquisition strategies are dictated by the prevailing circumstances in the age one lives; we can't expect what worked in the Stone Age to work in the medieval ages. Often times we say that something is out-dated or not in vogue, simply because it has been updated. Civilization and new inventions make change possible- both philosophical and material inventions. Rockefeller and his contemporaries in other fields of business were influenced by the spirit imbedded in the doctrines of *laissez-faire* capitalism which allowed people to carry out their business activities with little or no regulation from the government. Also imbued by the philosophy of social Darwinism as propounded by William Sumner, some business managers in that period believed that it was only the fittest that could survive in any business environment. They used aggressive strategies to pit themselves against those who abide by the ethics of business practice, and subsequently frustrated them into bankruptcy.

Each generation has the duty of defining what the will or essence of the age is, and set to actualize the purpose of its existence. In doing so, they strive to promote social policies that work to their advantage. For example, prior to industrial revolution agrarian societies particularly in Africa demonstrated that number was an integral part of economic production. The higher the number of children born in a family unit meant more productivity in cultivating the ground for food production. But with the emergence of mechanized farming or more appropriately, the advent of knowledge based economy; attention was shifted to increasing man's technological prowess. Knowledge or information driven economy is the reliance on experience to foster wealth.

In our time (digital age), technologies are deployed in various meaningful ways. Trade, for example, has taken a virtual dimension. It has become wide spread and has far reaching impacts than when you physically engage people in the streets or in their working places to market your products and services to them. It's more beneficial to society to operate in accordance with the dictates and circumstances of the time. Though our situations differ, it's ideal to adapt to the trends in a changing world, and key into its practices.

To understand this social milieu of economic development, let us consider the interactions between rich and poor. Everyone is useful as others. There could be outward differences but if you look inward it's only ideological differences; the one that appears more prosperous always take advantage of inward causes of wealth. These are kinds of wealth that are yet to be realized. They are repository of man's abilities- the ability to think smartly and the capacity to trade on exchangeable values. Wealth managers do not just think, they think about their thoughts. Thinking about how to acquire resources will not manifest unless we begin to think about how to improve our social and technical knowledge in the broad sense. Anyone that knows how to utilize the environment apparently understands the processes involved in wealth acquisition, whether he is educated or not. We cannot intone that Bachelor's degrees or certifications are the only route to wealth acquisition.

He who knows the underlying principles of his trade is an able thinking man- he possesses the ability required to produce wealth. His mental state determines how he acquires and manages wealth. When we see ourselves prospering before we prosper, we are boldly making statement that we are entrepreneurs. The impression we create in the mind of others about ourselves is often referred to as personal branding. Then, we find ourselves in a sitch where all we do is to interact with our ideas and the environment. Of course, beautiful ideas are viral or seductive by nature.

Entrepreneurship is therefore the wheel that drives beautiful ideas that have been mooted to generate wealth, especially when it is targeted at solving problems. One of the qualifications of an entrepreneur is his creativity, the ability to provide solutions and utilize economic resources for greater yield. Land and other natural resources are gifts of nature. But they have not independently helped to solve economic problems neither can they create social conditions that denote wealth. For many, making a choice as to which economic problem is to be prioritized is often a tight walk. Cognition is at the centre of entrepreneurship. Man is not just rational; he applies his mental faculties to identify useful resources and how to put them to proper use. He understands how to make the right economic choices. He also identifies opportunities and chooses the resources needed to tap into the opportunities. As long as we continue to detach human capacity to think from how wealth is acquired, the more our resources are being mismanaged.

If you consider Nigeria, the hallmark of misguided opportunities, you will see that she was a country without managerial leadership. There was oil boom in Nigeria in the 1970s. At that point, the problem of the country as proclaimed by one of her leaders wasn't money but how to spend it. Nigeria is a country in dire need of strong institutions and incorruptible leadership. She yearns for men and women of great ideas and capacity to manage her wealth efficiently. Nigeria like many African countries is rattled by the wealth of her natural resources. They would conclude that the resources are already there to cater for the needs of the citizens. Africa has failed to formulate policies, philosophies and abide by general behaviours that are in concomitant with economic growth. Unfortunately, selfishness, nepotism and corruption have become the continents' major setback. In general terms, Africa hasn't mustered the political will to create wealth that will benefit everyone. Most prosperous countries in the world do not have oil neither do they bank their hope on it. For them, investing on human capital or creativity is the key factor in wealth creation.

The more we rely on physical technologies without understanding wealth accumulation strategies, the less effective our capacity to develop and manage the resources will be. The demand of wealth creation as a process is that, to be really wealthy, it must begin by discovering ourselves and understanding where our strength and weakness lies. All men are equal in some respects but the wealth of our vision, specialized knowledge, skills and creativity has classified us.

Unfortunate religious generations have cried aloud unto God, blaming Him for everything. They are unfortunate because they are indoctrinated to believe that the church of God is where the daily bread is baked. They also believe that as natural disasters occur, God has forsaken them to suffer in penury- they pray and ask for their yoke of generational curse to be broken. I don't want to dwell on whether wealth is governed by divine will or not. I have earlier pointed out that our attitude to certain belief systems or reasoning influence our economic status. But like the voice in the bible, it was possibly asked upon the creation of the universe, "choose you today whom you will serve" and nature chose man. Although man is part of nature, he is the greatest beneficiary of its benevolence. Among the natural agents, he has the superior brain to exert control on others. His brain gives him the mental energy to learn, relearn and unlearn. Part of the training process lies in our ability to discover the role we can perform effectively. As the world moved to an industrialized economy in twentieth century, there was a need for continued training which paved way for upward career mobility, business growth and personal prosperity.

So we can conclude that nothing governs wealth more than the human will. Let's dabble into an imaginary situation now and imagine the impression of a modern entrepreneur if he travels to 19th century sprawling town in Sub- Saharan Africa. He will quipped rhetorically, "Why are people poor?" The towns achieves their relatively wellbeing from trade. The higher in quantity of the goods and demand, the higher returns they will make. That's their understanding of the economics of wealth acquisition. The lower class which comprises about 70 % of the population engage in tilling the lands. Education is not so important to them than their flourishing market.

While standing on one corner in a modern market therein, the entrepreneur will watch people as they buy their needs from one store to another. His eyes might range over dozens of people who are buying and selling goods. It won't take long for the eyes to fixate on a particular girl who is supposed to be in school at that hour of the day in other climes. He will, in his own summation, see a young promising girl with untapped potentials in a make -shift store waving the passers-by to come and buy petty wares she has sampled on the table. The out of school teenage girl enthusiastically calls out for customers. "While her persuasive prowess is unmatchable, her trading articles are commonly found in the market," we assume the entrepreneur will conclude. It is obvious her talent isn't employed in a remarkable degree.

It is illogical to understand why people are poor if you cannot figure out why they are rich. Now, the logic is this- wealthy men "look down" to understand what poor people pass through and so if the poor "looks up", he sees the inner workings of wealth. The understanding is deeply rooted in an economic background. The entrepreneur, for example, is affected by the problem he intends to solve- he can't benefit from a solution that never exists. It follows that those who have endured the abundant malice of poverty are eager to understand how the mechanism of wealth creation works, but will only do so when they are properly guided.

Assessment of the logic

Now, let us assess the potency of the logic I have been flaunting on in the previous pages. In doing so, we shall liken wealth, in a loose sense, to a rock: rocks undergo certain reactions by the effects of water, weather, biota, and so on before it is broken into small parts or smithereens. This process is what geologists call weathering. If rock naturally decomposes, it will be likened to hereditary wealth. Yet, it takes the ability of the beneficiaries to refine and put it into proper use. The reason is simply that large rocks cannot necessarily be moved without some mental and physical labour. We can draw some lessons from Newton's law of motion. Every object in a state of inertia tends to remain in the state unless an external force applies to it. It's a grave mistake for one to aspire to become wealthy without trying one's hand on something. An idle hand is an empty pocket and not just the devil's workshop. If you want to unveil a hidden treasure, you need to search your mind to find answers to where it could be before setting out to accomplish the goal. But if you remain in a state of inertia, you will never find it. The way we conceptualise wealth determines the kind of actions we need to take. In general terms, there are two choices before us. It's either we embrace our conditions as they present themselves or we become concerned with the power of our mind-set to shape the conditions.

My explanation is that wealth acquisition is a process, and even when wealth is inherited it needs our mental and physical efforts to amass more. This same effort is needed to manage it. A man who is lazy to plant in his farm won't dine when others are dining. If his ancestors have bequeathed a large farmland for him, he wouldn't depend on leased land. At first he feels like the Lord of Manor. That same feeling will cost him his inheritance if he fails to apply wisdom. Now, if he fails to make proper use of the farmland, he will starve.

Historically, the wealth of Egyptian dynasties was underpinned by the productive capacity of the Egyptian peasantry. Between 1250 and 1517 the Egyptian Fellahin, which is an Arabic word for peasantry were hereditary holders of their small family plots in the fertile flood plain of the Nile valley. Irrespective of the fact that a family plot was traditionally passed from one generation to another, any benefactor or fellahin who couldn't pay the levied tax was often expelled from his own plot of land. This way a fellah became slave if he failed to pay tax which was in advance imposed on all crops and domestic livestock. The peasants suffered a great deal under Mamluks.

Modern governments levy tax on wealth which may be another means of generating fund for the state and also provide certain amenities for the citizens. A progressive tax can reduce income inequality. Governments on their own part promise to cure societal problem, but most times they end up making certain groups or cronies rich overnight which stimulates economic instability in the long run. Despite the diverse positions of historians on the taxation system under Mamluks dynasty, the Egyptian case clearly shows the effect of complacency in pursuit of wealth.

The lesson for entrepreneurs is that when they set targets for a business without necessarily being under compulsion, the business will not fare better. There are obvious challenges that come with fortune. The saying that "What must be must be" is not applicable to wealth creation. If you refuse to think positively and work on your human relations, what must be, must be poverty, even amidst government promises to better the lives of the citizens. The wealth manager must see himself as a captain who directs the movement of a ship. Any slightest mistake on his part may cause the ship to capsize. Budding entrepreneurs should always be on alert so that in the event or wake of government's stringent policies that are not favourable to their enterprise, they will be able to control whatever panic that comes with it.

There would be need for entrepreneurs to share the burden of welfare in our society. A stiff reliance on government to provide employment for the teeming unemployed population is not the best way to go. The 21st century with its attendant innovations in technology witnessed a leap in new business ideas. I don't scoff being an employee of any sort in a government establishment. But if private owned businesses can be well managed than some government properties, it signifies that individual capacities to become independent provoke more abundance, and make them become free from financial worries. Wealth can be equated to a kite that needs human drive (labour and skills), initiatives (ideas and technologies) and external factors like wind (Gift of nature) to fly. Wealth is the aggregate of our positive thoughts and the culminating result of transforming those things we cherish into value.

As shown in my analysis, we can fancifully use weathering to describe the act of wealth creation. It doesn't matter if it's a chemical or mechanical process as in inherited wealth or wealth acquired through smartness; the import here is that wealth like a deposit of rocks can be tapped, harnessed and managed by the actions of man. Imagine what happens in a society where every girl at the age of the girl in an African market indulges in street hawking or solely embrace exchange of articles for money. The poor little girl would be better off with quality capacity building to use her persuasive ability, for instance, in more elaborate ways to make money. It therefore follows that all the riches and glory great men enjoy on earth are the output of their efforts to carve a niche for themselves while adopting the best practicable means to create wealth.

Entrepreneurs are managers of human and natural resources. Informed by their instincts and intellect, they perform the classical functions of management. They plan to avoid loss; they plan to gain profits, provide the required leadership, organize and control the resources at their disposal. The effort by which economic matters are advanced and established is couched on these tenets. When the cardinal principles are well practiced, business enterprises flourish, but when they are neglected the enterprises decline in growth. The point is that if the resources are not efficiently managed the economy will be in distress. There is only a thin grey line between an inefficient manager of resources and a crumbling economy. That line is called poverty. It's not enough to say that someone is poor or wealthy. We should view our status as the reflection of our state of mind.

If we are not mindful of the future, we will become complacent with our achievement. At the other hand, one man goes about managing his resources with prudence; the other man goes with lavishness. Prudence is the ability to assess the nature of your income. The assessment will guide you to avoid spending more than your earnings. A rich man who lavishes his wealth will soon beg for money.

Considering how the penetration of water or the decomposition organic materials into the ground either form rock or leave it with no choice than to crack, or transform it into oil and gas at certain temperatures and pressures, wealth is naturally irresistible to mankind. But most times we wrongly interpret wealth by ascribing it an unmerited veneer. If you attend a public ceremony in Africa where invited guests are expected to make donations, you will notice that the strength of their financial muscle is used as the primary factor to determine who should be invited to the high table. But sometimes they commit errors in distinguishing between the wealthy man and the money man. We must constantly remind ourselves as John Law explains that money doesn't constitute wealth. Money is a means of exchange. It can be changed for goods and services, or against a business. Wealth is derived from mental and labour exercises, and most importantly, it has the power to duplicate itself. What this means is that the outcome of wealth is determined by the social conditions it created. The number of currency notes or coins in your wallet does not constitute riches. Money can deplete out of spending; anyone that cannot manage his expenditures can hardly manage resources. As poverty is inimical to man, so is reckless spending to wealth. Wealth is like a flower that requires watering for it to grow, and when it grows it keeps asking for pruning. It's expedient to establish more streams for generating income in accordance with extant laws of the land. Man as a rational being tries his hand in profitable enterprises to open doors for more streams of income.

Application of the logic
What I have been discussing in this chapter doesn't require knowledge of economics to apply the

logic. The capacity to create steady self-sustaining income is a prerequisite for investments. Most times, moments and events provide us the opportunity to start up something new asides our immediate job. Business oriented minds look out for opportunities everywhere.

I will use Jack Ma, the founder of the popular e-commerce company known as Alibaba to draw my extrapolation on this. Ma didn't waste his money on adventures. As a Chinese English teacher, he developed interest in the Internet venture during a visit to the United States in 1995. In e-commerce, he saw bountiful business opportunities. In 1999, he led 18 people to host their own site in 1999.

In 2004, the company gained the largest initial public offer (IPO) in history at $ 25 billion. In considering how Jack Ma was able to break into the e-commerce industry, it's important to note that he thoroughly examined the business environment in China, and therefore came up with the aim of connecting Chinese manufacturers directly to foreign importers. The big lesson here is that if you want to stand out, you must not imitate a business pattern *in toto*. It is safer to allow the business to shape your ideas. Jack Ma allowed his knowledge of the business realities in China to stray from American e-commerce business model. He never had any technical or business skills. Yet one of the preconditions of his success was that he banked on the knowledge of what could become the fate of internet business in the nearest future to invest in Alibaba.

Next to this lesson is the knowledge of not putting your eggs in one basket. Successful business men are good at this practice. They keep expanding their cash flows.

The story of the market girl in this chapter is best understood by realizing that the first thing that should occupy our thoughts is to discover the power of human will. Self-discovery goes a long way to determine your wealth creation path.

The changeover from traditional ways of running the market system to modern markets reminds us of the need to always adapt to changes. Leveraging your specialized knowledge and showing the capacity for increasing your ability to take the advantage of your gifts, and the overall comprehension of the changing market environment, gives you control over wealth. Right now, God is asking you –what do you know? Whatever your answer is, that's what you possess.   I

CHAPTER TWO

WEALTH AND SOCIETY

The cock that crows in the morning belongs to one household but his voice is the property of the neighbour-hood- Chinua Achebe

Man possesses potential immense wealth in his mental ability. He can moot a thousand and one ideas on wealth creation models. When he fails to deploy those fundamental resources to affect society positively, the standard of living will be undermined. To promote public weal, just like the cock that crows early in the morning, he transforms his abilities into labour which in turn creates wealth for society.

Conversely, any government that cannot set a template for the state's economic prosperity is set to undermine welfarism. Such state is poor to the optics of society, irrespective of, say the degree of its Gross Domestic Product per capita and the Gross National Product which are used as metrics for evaluating her economic performance. We should be reluctant to draw conclusions on the development of a state based on impressive economic calculus or statistical results which do not necessarily eradicate poverty. This does not invalidate the significance of statistics as a viable tool in determining whether an economy is growing or contracting. But the common man in the street doesn't understand these barometers or statistical appraisals.

What an average person is interested in is to see how clear-cut government policies would contribute in driving out poverty, diseases and reduction in mortality rate. He is convinced by what he sees than what he hears. Clearly, wealth which has not played any role in their life cannot be meaningful. It doesn't make any sense, for instance, to celebrate a healthy GDP in a country where people lost their job on daily basis. Loss of job breeds poverty. The labour force of a thriving economy enjoys job security that can reach certain level of life satisfaction. We may very well have a situation where we praise our economic achievements and turn a blind eye on the things that matter to society- the financial freedom of the majority.

The Entrepreneur who sets to build a flourishing business empire, or to generate wealth for the society, or to become richly comfortable is just seeking to achieve those objectives. But they do not consciously seek to influence how the society chooses to benefit from the wealth. There is a recent example my memory won't fail me to give. In 2011 Aliko Dangote the Nigerian born business mogul was declared Forbes' richest man in Africa. The report rated him richer than Mark Zuckerberg, the founder of Facebook. But when I noticed the euphoria that greeted the news that Dangote was richer than Zuckerberg, I began to think differently. Individuals who engage in wealth appraisals or ratings should concern themselves with the peculiarity of such wealth to every group in the society- no such wealth exist to appeal the general public. Each group prefer to celebrate wealth that is more favourable to their own economic conditions and aspirations. In North Africa, the comparison wasn't so much important. Facebook was one of the core stimuli that facilitated the mobilization of the 21st century political revolution in North Africa popularly known as Arab Spring.

It's remarkable that the Forbes report came at a time when Tunisia, Egypt and Libya were passing through sweeping political trials which resulted in revolutionary movements. In Egypt, Facebook exemplifies Adam Smith's celebrated statement that in pursuing his own advantage, each individual was "led by an invisible hand to promote an end which was not part of his own intention." Zuckerberg might not have envisaged the kind of influence Facebook exerts on almost every sphere of our lives as it does today. The world has become more cohesive and globalized than ever through Facebook and other genres of social media. It provides advertisement funnels for businesses. Despite the negative sides of the evolving technologies, the multi functionalities of social media have allowed new marriages, contacts and information to be disseminated. It also exposes the ills in the society. Those who don't see the opportunities wealth creators provide still wallow in ignorance. In business sphere, Facebook provides far - reaching marketing strategies for entrepreneurs.

Zuckerberg would be hailed in North Africa for providing the technological platform which helped to keep the masses abreast of the political developments. It aided the coordination of the movement that invariably stimulated the political consciousness of a million in Egypt. It was the pressure it inspired that brought about the protest against unemployment, poverty and the visible corruption among the government circles in Egypt. However, the main target was the rule of Hosni Mubarak, who had been in power for thirty years.

A Swahili proverb says that lack of money doesn't necessarily mean being poor. The result of the uprising may not have directly filled their pockets with money as it's not much important in this analogy. What matters is that people are more concerned with wealth that has duplicating or life changing effects. At any material time, those who profit from the opportunities provided by wealth creators can't be said to be poor. The effects of economic statistics or ratings should reflect on our standard of living and peaceful coexistence. Entrepreneurship is functional and we need to understand, to a quantifiable degree, it functions in a society.

The cognitive orientation of the entrepreneur, his passion and interest form the fulcrum upon which he conceives his ideas which later translate to services and products. His understanding of the situation, namely politics (changes in government policies and laws), economy, environment, culture, etc., enables him to choose what to invest in. Then he would set his goals. The goals clearly show what the manager intends to achieve; providing solutions or influence. For example, the need for a more cohesive society and common ground where global interactions would take place might have featured prominently in Mark Zuckerberg's goals. In other words, the goals of the manager depend on the situations of the end users or consumers. The impact of any service or product makes in a particular society is determined by the category of people whose patronage it enjoys.

Another consideration is the perception of the society about the goods and services. Societal perception of a particular product informs how they respond or react to it. They either embrace it wholeheartedly or lukewarmly accept it, or give suggestions. Entrepreneurs should always create a communication system between them and the consumers. This factor is very important to wealth manager because it gives him information he needs to evaluate on the drawing board. It provides him with ample ideas as it concerns how to improve on the production of goods or services.

The contradictions inherent in measuring wealth that does not reflect on the lives of groups in society have been discussed. Now, it remains for me to discuss the factors that can boost wealth in particular societies. I admire the Singaporean example. Lee Kuan Yew, the prime minister of Singapore from 1965 to 1991 has in his book titled *Singapore: From Third World to First World* explained how he brought practicable policies to bear on the country's economic life. In considering the far reaching impacts of Yew's economic policies, I think if a state like ours does not wish to be punctuated by poverty, it should embrace some of these factors that spark growth and development.

National peace

Peace is deemed a vital component required of a country to develop. It is attained if a government is devoted to people's welfare instead of oppressing them. Peace and prosperity are like umbilical cord. Holistically, a country whose government is corrupt and lacks political will finds it difficult to live in peace. A country where the rule of law is undermined, the system of government is bound to suffer- checks and balances will be suffocated. Where there is no peace, there will be social and economic unrest, prompting destructive criticism on the government of the day. In such situation, everyone laments bitterly. And a section of the populace would want to pull down the government.

Yew was therefore justified in keeping Singapore out of internal or external warfare. Understanding that war drains the state's treasury, he opted for non-alignment in her foreign policy milieu. Any country that engages in major conflicts internally or externally is bound to encounter losses.

All inclusive policies on all sections of the society

In a multi - ethnic society, the government shouldn't marshal its economic policies to favour any particular ethnic group than others. Singapore is an example of a society with racial presence. Yet Lee Kuan Yew in his narratives saw the masses as a people and not as racial groups.

As I have said elsewhere, government must make the environment conducive for private sector to float. A coordinated effort of citizens irrespective of their ethnic leanings is the backbone of national development. To achieve this goal government must equitably empower their citizens; everyone needs to have access to education and employment. This approach will in no small measure help to maintain a cohesive society where people thrive to live a meaningful life. Leaders should be committed to address economic and social challenges as a whole burden, and not to be selective in that regard.

Education

Education is the process of training the mind to think deeply in other to solve problems. Both formal and informal education is very instructive for development and growth in any giving society. Public orientation and acquisition of skills will certainly reduce the crime rate and lawlessness in the state; education gives hope to the future of society.

A Political System that Allows the Spirit of Enterprise to Blossom

Paradoxically, the experience of developing countries provides clear evidence that abundance of raw materials and huge labour do not wholly create wealth. If not why are countries with fewer natural resources more developed than their counterparts with rich natural endowments? The case of Singapore shows that a population with the spirit of enterprise creates wealth. Government must provide an enabling environment for individual capacity to develop well organized business ventures, and thereby take a leap upwards. Governments with strong institutions fare better than those with abundant natural resources. For example, an organized banking system is a plus for the growth of the economy. Both government and financial institutions should make policies that favour entrepreneurship. Entrepreneurship is an integral part of a strong economy. I don't need to bother you with the story of how private sectors transformed the Japanese economy during the era of Meiji restoration - it was simply phenomenal.

The spirit of enterprise was also evident in the making of America. J. P. Morgan, a strong financier was able to save the United States during the economic panic of 1907.He had earlier rescued America out of a financial pickle in 1894. But for our conversation, I'm mostly particular about his 1907 effort with its lessons. The 1907 economic crisis began as a result of negligence on the part of companies handling wills and Estates, who exploited the legal loopholes in American system to become spectators in the stock market. The investments didn't augur well, and thereby caused the collapse of the trusts. In that circumstance, the American financial system was badly threatened.

Morgan stepped in as America's de factor central bank primarily because none existed at that time, but importantly, the financial crisis that almost turned into economic depression begged for a helper which he readily presented himself. Despite the fact that President Roosevelt wasn't in good terms with Morgan because of his involvement in big businesses, he gave him the concession to assemble his fellow financiers to push money into America New York's banking and other weak financial institutions. If you recall, Morgan's intervention in the crisis revealed the weakness in American financial system, and was instrumental in the establishment of U.S.A Federal Reserve in 1913.

Provision of social amenities

In 2016 the United Nations estimated that about 2.4 billion people in the world lack access to basic sanitation services such as toilets or latrines. In that report, each day nearly 1,000 children die due to preventable water and sanitation related diarrheal diseases. You can see how some states find it difficult to moot lofty ideas to tackle the challenges of making clean water accessible to the people; poverty of ideas which results in denying the masses befitting social conditions.

Now, let us see how poverty is perceived at the individual level. At this point, to become POOR means Passing over Opportunities Repeatedly. Why do we borrow money to solve monetary problems and fail to pay back as and when due? Those who are capable of servicing their debt but refuse to do so are not only greedy, they constantly misuse opportunities. Our view of poverty, regardless of any speculative belief system is that it is not a curse but a cause to shake off every shackle of poor mentality.

From the above insight, the question we need to ask is *why are some people more prosperous than others?* I may not be able to give a straight jacketed answer to this because prosperity is costly. But if we appreciate some of the causative factors of poverty at the individual level, we can then provide some answers. So for my analysis not to be superficial, we should look at the minor causes of poverty at individual level.

1. Free gift is always mistaken as a trap, and most times individuals rely heavily on what they will receive from the rich. They always want to be given fish not minding that it's important to learn not only how to fish but how to own a fish pond.

2. Individuals do not understand that a tap dropping water in the morning will fill a bucket to the brim in the evening. They think that if they start small they won't grow in the long run. Hence, they are always desperate to make quick money. The dictum has always been, "Do not despise your little beginning."

3. They are afraid to try new things. Starting up something new could be cumbersome but the end pays a great deal. Those who are sceptical to try something new remain stagnant. When you ask a poor man to start up something he will confess that he hasn't done it before, as if he had seen an

edifice that nobody erected. It was Vincent Van Gogh who said:

If you hear a voice within you saying" you are not a painter ", by all means paint and the voice will be silenced.

There is no harm if one tries one's hand on a novel project, but those who choose to remain poor will always harbour fears to engage in a new enterprise. Take your time and think of a legitimate means of generating cash -flows, then go for it. We live in the age where there are result oriented business models. If the traditional ways of doing business are not more choosable, there is a paradigm shift in the way today's businesses are conducted. All you need to do is to get in touch with the contemporary realities and profit from them.

4. Most people are poor because they don't associate with great minds. Instead of them to get the opinion of entrepreneurs on pecuniary issues they surround themselves with people who are as helpless as they are. Have you seen where a blind man leads blind people? The kind of people you relate with shapes your line of thoughts. So if you have big dreams why don't you get in touch with people that share the same goal with you?

5. A poor man doesn't know what he wants. Ask him what he can do to make money, he would say anything goes. He has no choice as to discover where his strength lies. What this means is that while wealth managers have a clear vision of what they want to achieve, poor men do not set goals. Even when they plan for the future, they don't usually have the plan. In this case, they allow the future to control itself instead of being instrumental in shaping what tomorrow brings forth.

Why does poverty persist?

People have asked me why poverty exists while there are wealthy men. It is a generalized question asked in a bad taste. The right question would have been, "why does poverty persist amidst plenty?"

To the first question there can be no conclusive answer, for the motive behind the actions of men is highly different and personal. For instance, in Africa the notion of "helping hands" is well and alive. Foreign donors through various agencies and governments often come to the people's aid. There is also the tendency for people to ask for help from friends and families. But wealthy men may grudgingly refuse to help on their own volition. Yet, the refusal or the mockery or the sarcastic jabs the rich would occasionally pelt on the downtrodden ordinarily contribute to richness of the poor. Not every rich possesses the gift of giving, or understands what it means to help others grow. But don't despise the rich because he fails to lend a helping hand- strive to break away from poverty. There must be something to learn from a rich man; his triumphs and mistakes will guide you to prosper. Studying what the rich does and how he does it is a source of help on itself.

Moreover, men generally guide their self-esteem jealously. Self-centered rich men depend on the loyalty or patronage of their followers. They devise means by which the followers always come to them for petty help. The reason for his action is that if he establishes the poor, he fears they won't be loyal to him. He derives satisfaction for being consulted whenever they need money.

Since the first question is what bothers people very often, I would say that it's important for people who seek financial help to carefully reflect on the motives of those who help them. If it's not based on the need to make them financially independent, but rather to make them depend on their wealth, it is worth re-examination. The irony of the whole thing is that wealthy men are quick to forget that in time of adversity, none of their loyalists whom they have not empowered would make any financial promise. Entrepreneurs should try and establish people because when the chips are down they will enjoy the wealth for a second time. Albert Pine was right when he said:

What we do for ourselves dies with us, what we do for others and the world remains, and are immortal.

Now, the real issue is that poverty persists because we lack ideas. Most importantly, it is pervasive in a society where self-serving culture thrives. No matter how it is overstretched to portray that wealth is self -serving, or tailored to the advantage of a few in society, its impacts are far reaching. For instance, entrepreneurs solve the problem of unemployment in a fashionable nostrum. Think about this - Entrepreneurs create employment and provide wealth creation models for other businesses to thrive. It's a challenge for the downtrodden to stand up and unleash their potentials in order to lead society to prosperity. An example is provided by the rag to rich story of Cornelius Vanderbilt. He dropped out of school at the age of eleven and persuaded his mother to loan him 100 USD. It was this money that he used to start a ferry business. We were told that he repaid the loan with an additional 1,000 USD one year later.

If my generation cannot reasonably moot beautiful ideas that can drag us to the top, we are mentally poor. We would lose count of wealthy men who were not born with silver spoon. So entrepreneurship is something we must encourage to sound the death knell to poverty by providing the healing balm that will cushion the adverse effects of poverty. Entrepreneurs profit from the experience of the past ones while seeking to solve new problems. Bearing this in mind, it is immaterial to stop trying even when failure has been recorded in the previous attempts. We are our choice and what we become.

CHAPTER THREE

INFLUENCE OF WEALTH ON MANKIND

Remember that there is nothing stable in human affairs; therefore, avoid undue elation in times of prosperity, or undue depression in times of adversity - Socrates

Adam Smith defines wealth in his work- An Enquiry into the Nature and Causes of the Wealth of Nations (Book I, Chapter II) as "natural products that have been secured, moved, combined, separated, or in other ways modified by human exertion, so as to fit them for the gratification of human desires." Elsewhere, succeeding neo-classical Economists have argued that the definition elevated wealth as the only important factor in human society while neglecting human qualities or activities as other sources of satisfying human desires. For them, material goods cannot satisfy human wants alone. And if we believe this assertion to be true, materialism cannot therefore be said to be the only outcome of wealth acquisition. Orthodox economists classified labour into productive and unproductive kinds. They consider services unworthy of productivity, but failed to realize that the service of a poet, for example, can also gratify one's desire. Wealth means different things to different people. Yet, the thrust of my argument in chapter one is that man emerges as the decisive factor in conception of wealth- his mental labour appears paramount. Every human endeavour is directly or indirectly productive. Our mental ability to discern the usefulness of human efforts would convert them into economic materials.

The things we don't understand mean nothing to us until someone gives meaning to its nothingness or nihilism. My story of shepherd and flocks points to this conclusion. The shepherd represents managers while flocks are classed as wealth. As a lad I grew up with the knowledge that my paternal grandmother whom I never met had flocks. She was in the business of giving out some of the flocks in order to make profit. For each sheep my grandmother gave out, she had a share in its lamb, which she would in turn give out or sale to recompense her efforts. I had the vaguest idea of how to rear sheep, while my grandma's "enterprise" continued to thrive upon her demise.

The shepherd, in the morning, takes the flocks to pastoral scene where they graze on growing grass. In the afternoon, he would relocate them to an untouched grass land; grass is a useful commodity to shepherds- it enhances production because if the flocks don't feed well they wouldn't live to reproduce. So the essence of this rotational flock grazing strategy is to enable the sheep feed more satisfactorily till the day gets a little dark. Then, he would take them home as they match in an organized rank. He takes care of the sheep, and won't mistakenly make a noose out of the thread he uses to pen the sheep, and to the grazing field. If he does so he may leave and return only to find out that the sheep has given up the ghost. No wise manager will carelessly push his enterprise to the precipice. He takes precautions in all he does. At home, he can find other eatables like fibre and give to each of them to munch. The flocks bleat with joy having satisfied their stomach all day.

Now, while lying down happily in their pen they would be busy regurgitating or bringing up the food from their rumen before they would now slowly re-chew and swallow it. But during the dry season when all the greenish plants in the field have dried up, they would bleat in agony. Left alone, it cannot plant grasses or save for the time of adversity. If it goes astray, it will be exposed to dangerous animals in the bush or trespass on somebody's farmland, and may not survive the consequences. So the loud bleating continues until it attracts the attention of the shepherd who goes and gathers plenty fodder for their consumption.

Wealth looks attractive to everyone because man has been naturally posited to become aware of the implications of poverty - the typical sheepish starvation and deprivation. The story of Shepherd enables us to understand what happens if man fails to exert influence on wealth. At the other hand, wealth exerts influence on human's affairs to the extent that we show an increasing capacity to survive by utilizing the environment.

We have seen the quest of man to earn more and more money as if wealth amounted to everything. But to say that wealth can fulfil all things is to allude that man is solely an economic being. Igbo speaking tribe in Nigeria believe that good reputation is more precious than gold (wealth). How does the love for wealth points to explain the reality that not everyone who possesses multiple digits in his bank accounts is fulfilled in life? To clinch the argument, there are many rich men who do not have inner peace, happiness and respect for mankind. It is obvious that money cannot buy these things. So beyond acquisition of wealth, there are other things that make life complete. While money can buy bed, it can't buy sleep. Wealth can't stop a man whose fate has destined to join his appointed path from   dying. Though wealth is not everything, it is very useful. If you are in a situation where the choice is between buying someone a beer and giving him money, the second choice will be the best bet- it could solve him a problem.

In our time, priests would ask the congregation to bring unto the Lord, gifts and tithes. He pleads that the church's edifice needs to be formidable. Decent men and women of goodwill, instead, bring plenty of money to raise new foundations. "That's the wonders of God exemplified by men of faith", the priest would say as he prays for the cheerful givers. And those who are yet to give are asked to repent from their sin. The only sin those "men of church" have committed is that they are poor. But rebuilding the house of God and repairing its ruins goes beyond remodelling its physical structures. Our body is the temple of God. We owe it to God to retrace our bad steps, and obey His codes. Those in need should be helped out and not to be cursed. The church should live by example by showing compassion to members of the congregation.

Our general understanding of the usefulness of wealth informs why from time immemorial, it is difficult not to find a big man in every town of the world. From the great Mansa Musa of ancient Mali to our modern time Bill Gates, we saw men who bestrode the corridors of wealth like colossus in their respective domains with commitment to philanthropy. While in each town everybody strives to build a stupendous fortune, it's unholy to be controlled by wealth.

Some wealthy men use their resources to intimidate those who don't have. They bribe their way through virtually everything. It gives them disgusting confidence. You see them easily talk down on others. This category of people becomes the butt of many jokes whenever they are struck by tragedy. This is so because they allow money to have undue negative influence on them. On the positive flip of the influence, a wealth manager improves his life style; he is mindful of what he eats, the way he walks, talks and he is poised to garner more knowledge that will be impactful in society. Generally, he lives a healthy life style and does not discriminate between rich and poor.

On the path of wealth acquisition, one must acquire the requisite virtues to sustain the pace and sustain one's achievements. It requires self-discipline, vision, perseverance and the spirit of reverence. On the last virtue, Plato, a renowned Greek philosopher, admonished parents to bequeath to their children not riches but the spirit of reverence. We also read in the Bible how King Solomon asked God for wisdom and not riches. Apparently, when his prayer was granted, every other thing including wealth was added unto him. The big lesson here is that fortune or its inheritance shouldn't rob us of those values we hold in high esteem as a people. It does not make sense to over pamper- it will result to stubbornness. States that spend enormous time obsessing about wealth with little or no effort at strengthening the institutions of the State end up being poorer, while public officials and their cronies grow richer day by day. It results in the concentration of wealth in the hands of small percentage of the population. This attitude does not only breed corruption, it reduces the states to a structurally weak ones. According to Martin Luther King:

To be free, you have to learn to give up the love of wealth and the fear of death. If you are not anxious for money nobody can buy you off, if you are not afraid of death nobody can scare you off.

Wealth is designed to be controlled by man, and not a sort of instrument to control the sensibilities of men. Another illustration points to this conclusion. Nicholas II who was one the wealthiest men in his time as the ruler of Russia could not consolidate the efforts of his predecessors. His rule from 1894 was marked with incessant unrest until he was forced to abdicate in the Russian Revolution of 1917 by the Bolsheviks. It was under his rule that Russia was humiliated by Japan in Russo-Japanese war despite his accumulated wealth. At the individual level, Nicholas II was able to eradicate material poverty but he failed woefully to get rid of the poverty of statecraft. Thus, his ineptitude in statecraft or as some Historians would say, his stupidity cost him his leadership position because he was not able to pilot the affairs of the state to an enviable lofty height.

Hence, to align with Plato's thought, Nicholas II was an example of someone whose parents bequeathed riches and not the spirit of reverence. He failed to respect the citizen's rights to economic and social inclusion. In general terms, a leader who seeks public office to acquire material things or promote self above the state, clearly betray the state's agenda. The things wealth cannot influence are left under our control.

We have heard a lot about the second coming of Jesus Christ. But I fear that if Jesus comes again he will be astonished to see the gap between the poor and the rich in our society. Christ, out of pity, after seeing the hiatus may still want to die for the sake of the rich- to redeem their sins. One of American entrepreneurs, Andrew Carnegie (1835-1919) stated that wealth is not to feed our egos, but to feed the hungry and to help people help themselves. In his famous essay, *The Gospel of Wealth* published in 1889, Carnegie wrote that wealth should be distributed to promote welfare of other people and enrich society. There are people who have all the riches in the world but are at the centre of exploiting others. They find it difficult to give back to the society because they don't understand what it means to engage in commanding wealth. But men of value give more than they receive to inspire and affect lives positively, just like Carnegie did.

In all honesty, apart from the philanthropic gestures of the very rich men at looking into other people's eyes for assistance, I do not think it's apposite to praise the generosity of government authorities in providing welfare in their respective states as an act of charity. Ideally, a responsive government does not deserve special accolades for distributing state's values to her citizens who have surrendered their rights to the authority in expectant of good governance. The wealth of nations should be used for the purpose it's meant for, namely provision of public good. The citizens of developing countries have remained at the mercy of corrupt regimes and continually wallow in abject poverty.

The time for new narratives is now. The best way to tell the story is to reduce the rate at which we depend on government for survival. We must build the capacity to become sales persons where ideas are the trading articles, which both the government and the citizens will patronize. For instance, emerging interests in technology-based businesses haven't been fully tapped. Our growing understanding of science has enabled us to devise tools and technologies to carry out work easier. An entrepreneur has the ability to feed a hungry man and provide solutions to problems with regard to his own interest.

CHAPTER FOUR

HOW IS WEALTH ACQUIRED?

If you shape your life according to nature, you will never be poor; if according to people's opinions you will never be rich - Seneca

Before the middle of sixteenth century, Portugal and Spain had monopolized access to over-sea's wealth. But between 1520 and 1530 it was first challenged by France. King Francis of France 1 reacted to the monopoly with the following rhetorical question:

The sun shines on me just as on other: and I should like to see the clause in Adam's will that cuts me out from my share of the New World.

In a nutshell, it's your birth right to become rich. No class of people has the monopoly to make wealth or possess the exclusive right to become rich. Nobody can deprive you your right to become wealthy as long as you do not infringe on other people's rights. It is the kind of question King Francis 1 asked that spurs us into wealth acquisition. All the wealth men have flaunted in the past or the one they enjoy today is either genuine or gotten out of ruthlessness, or through other means.

To make money is a business of choice and not a feeling. People are driven to their destiny by their curiosity or enquiries. In the process of self-discovery, we seek to know many things about ourselves. If Michael Jackson could sing and dance well, what could have stopped him from making money? Jay-jay Okocha was able to dribble past everyone on a fine football pitch and smiled to the bank, you too should have a skill or something to sale- it must not be a tangible item. But I have not seen anyone who says he is poor because he doesn't have any skill or talent, or something to monetize. Man chooses his path. He rises and falls, and sometimes he remains stagnant. The truism is that the type of decisions we make in life determines where we stand in the lever.

We shall now examine various means through which man acquires wealth.

HERIDITARY WEALTH

Prefer knowledge to wealth, for one is transitory, the other perpetual - Socrates

This is an already established wealth, and all it requires is maintenance. It is a great privilege accorded to a manager by his parents. It gives him an edge over self-made wealth that takes a while to materialize.

Those who inherit wealth should not neglect the way the enterprise was run by the benefactor. They must be prudent enough to invest and spend wisely. But he must adapt to the policies of the prevailing business environment for him to succeed in holding unto the resources. Good managerial skills are the key factor in keeping any family business afloat. William Henry Vanderbilt, for example, who died in 1885 as the richest man in the world, inherited his wealth from his father Cornelius Vanderbilt. He was groomed by his father to become a business man, and he succeeded in expanding the family's railroad empire. Unfortunately, William's children were not able to manage one the celebrated fortunes in the gilded age.

The fact is that those who inherited their wealth have reasons to worry. Evidence of this abounds in our contemporary society. If they do not bring innovations into the business, the wealth will gradually disappear in a competitive business world. There is an adverse effect on wealth in absence of capable hands that would manage it. The reign of Basil II from 976 to 1025 was seen by Historians as the apex of the Middle Byzantine Empire because he was able to annex Bulgaria thereby making the empire the largest and strongest it had ever been in five centuries. Unfortunately, he had no heir to inherit his wealth, and the Byzantine Empire crumbled within half a century of his death.

In any case, the circumstances surrounding one's birth does not necessarily determine his economic status in the long run. Meritocracy is fast enthroning aristocracy in the social stratification. It's not only the children of the rich that have more chance to make it in life. If it happened in the time of John Rockefeller, it can happen in our own time. John grew up a hardworking man and became extraordinary rich despite the fact that he wasn't born into a rich family. You can be that rich man you want to be. Your family background doesn't pose any economic barrier on your way. If you look into the seeds of time, you would agree that change is truly constant. We must challenge ourselves to understand the changing trends in the world and apply it appropriately to our everyday life and actions.

In the past, people work hard to ascend to the class of wealthy men. Hard work means to go above board in attending to your duty call or task. But today it requires not only that you work hard but your smartness is a prerequisite for you to become wealthy. Today, smartness has reduced the stress people face in their business endeavours as most business organizations are now technologically driven. Businesses are now incorporated and operated online. Smart people are smart because they are able to solve problems and solve them quickly.

WEALTH ACQUIRED THROUH TACTICAL AND CALLOUS MEANS
The gods have placed upon earth two judges of human actions: conscience and history- Lord Acton

This is a typical example of when someone becomes rich at the detriment of others. The nexus between treachery and wealth creation can be created as an illicit and immoral picture. Most African societies prefer good reputation to wealth. Indulging in vices can bring prosperity; it can also ruin a man. It's wise to preserve one's life and posterity than to move towards self-destruction in the guise of making money. Barclays bank stands tall in London today but it was the loot two brothers, David and Alexander Barclay derived from slave trade in 1756 that was used to set up the bank. Cecil Rhodes the man in whose name Rhodesia the present day Zimbabwe was named after, imitated Barclays, and thus he forcefully invaded Southern Africa where he robbed the people of their gold and eventually became a young millionaire.

In March 2015 students of Cape Town University in South Africa began series of protest to remove the statue of Rhode which stood on the campus. The statue later fell in April. It shows that actions of the past live in the conscience of men. Those who adopt exploitation as their best means of wealth creation only succeed in laying a spiteful legacy. Despite the fact that Cecil John Rhodes died in 1920, ninety five years after, his ugly past haunted him posthumously. Politicians often hoodwink the electorates to believe that once they are elected into their respective government positions they would eradicate poverty, build bridges where they don't exist and erect such infrastructures that would ultimately salvage our economic woes. Surprisingly, they win our votes and amass wealth to themselves without fulfilling their campaign promises. These people and their cronies become rich over night while hands full of their subjects starve day and night.

Let us have a look at what happened in Mossack Fonseca a few years ago. Mossack Fonseca is the world's fourth biggest offshore law firm which was designed to incorporate companies in off shore jurisdictions, administers offshore firm for a fee and manage people's wealth. As at the time of gathering materials for this book, the company revealed the greatest ever leak of data in the world. The documents known as Panama papers contained information on the numerous ways in which wealthy people exploit secretive off shore tax regimes or havens. Though it's not illegal if someone saves offshore provided the source of the wealth is genuine, but if leaders had invested the stashed capital in their home countries, they would have facilitated national development and also pay taxes which of course goes back into other developmental strides. No citizen would be denied the impact of such investment on the state's economy. Money laundering or the act of keeping capital (sort of capital flight) away from home enables politicians to short-change the common wealth of their state at the detriment of the masses- whether rich or poor.

I have given examples of leaders who rose to power with the primary goal of feasting on what Nigerians would call the national cake- the wealth of the nation. I will now discuss other ways people on their own self-promotion extract obnoxious means in pursuing wealth. Some use gun, some use charms- yahoo plus, while others use their intellect. Now, let's examine the character of swindlers to generally have a better understanding of how people base their wealth acquisition on deception. A swindler, while trying to delude his victim, conceals his intentions. His focus is to capture the mind of that gullible fellow. He chooses a devious format that will take his victim unaware of his true dispositions. His formats are endless. He switches over to another whenever he dictates leakages. But being vulnerable or falling into the trap of swindlers doesn't in its entirety suggest that someone is weak. It is possible that the victim is greedy, lazy or that he wants to become rich by all means, and very fast too. In practice, a lot of people have used this guise to build wealth. A wise man cannot fall prey to their antics. He knows that any transaction that shuns openness, and in which decisions are quickly made is utmost suspicious.

Let me give another example of how other wealth managers organized themselves to eliminate competition in the market and thereby rose to prominence in business world. J.P.Morgan invested in financial and industrial empires which were built on an organization that dictated how interests are shared among competitors. The outcome of that initiative was an agreement with the competitors to divide the market into territorial monopolies. For example, Andrew Carnegie faces his steel industry and remained atop. We saw how the "gang-up" led to the production of a syndicate that fixed prices and outputs and fleeced the people, of course, through the wheels of capitalism. In their quest to remain atop in the business, they thrived to eliminate any twinge of conscience that will hinder it.

SYSTEMATIC APPROACH TO WEALTH CREATION
Intelligence without ambition is a bird without wings - Salvador Dali
Most super- rich in our society started from the scratch. Systemic approach to wealth creation involves short term and long term wealth creation strategies. It's the opposite of get rich quick syndrome. Man has been accustomed to earn a living from struggling for relevance and thriving to survive against hunger and deprivation. In this way there has been a deep sense of discovering one's inert abilities. Those abilities can be increased by acquiring education. Education teaches us two things; how to make a living and how to live. Education can be seen as a catalyst to increasing our understanding of how things around us work, or ought to work. However, it doesn't in itself guarantee success. Take for instance; Bill Gates who failed some of his subjects and couldn't finish his education has in his payroll, Engineers and notable graduates as his employees in Microsoft. Thomas Edison who invented electric bulb had only primary education. Yet, he was able to invent what graduates couldn't achieve at that time. Success can be achieved when your skills are rightly

utilized.

As I pointed out elsewhere, a man who knows his trade is as important as the educated man. The critical question here is why is a taxi driver, an artisan, a musician or a business man important as a professor? The answer is found in the imperatives to satisfy mutual economic needs. Individual specialization in areas they can stretch their skills to the max leads to complementarities of services which in turn create wealth. It's almost impossible for everyone to become lawyers or doctors. But it's possible for everyone to distinguish himself in his endeavours or chosen field. Martin Luther King in the following quote nicely validates this line of thought:

If a man is called to be a street sweeper, he should sweep streets even as Michelangelo painted, or Beethoven composed music, or Shakespeare composed poetry. He should sweep streets so well that all the hosts of heaven and earth will pause to say, there lived a great sweeper who did his job well

When we were growing up, our parents admonished us not to be lazy. In their own words, we should do those things required of a successful society when our contemporaries are doing them; if they start going to school you join them, if they are building or buying houses, you should do as well, and if they start getting married, by all means try and marry.

There are visible stages in life; from the time a baby is born, he crawls, and with great effort he learns how to stand and gradually he would attempt some walking steps. When you cross stage one, you move to another level. At some point, it was a common practice for those who didn't have the opportunity to go to school among the Igbo people of Nigeria to become apprentices in various trades. After an agreed number of years, their masters will settle them with some money to start up their own trade. If you reluctantly refuse to walk when others are walking, soon they will walk past you. You may want to fly, but unfortunately you have got no wings. Then, the only option left is to indulge in obnoxious acts of creating wealth, which is devoid of any known systematic process.

Wealth manager creates wealth gradually on the basis of the principle of compound interest on a long term plan. As the money you rightly invested grows, it compounds in itself and grows more with the passage of time. In other words, systematic investment on your skills yields proceeds in the long run. The great Zik of Africa, Nnamdi Azikiwe factored in wealth as his top priority while going to study in America in the early 1940s. The driving force , which he trusted will make him wealthy was to become intellectually formidable; to equip himself with the best tool known to mankind(education) and to participate in his country's political life. His investment in education aided his struggles for Nigeria's independence. The rewards for this bold step were riches, fame and great repute. If Zik had betrayed his purpose, he wouldn't have been successful. Broadly speaking, the bedrock of systematic approach to wealth creation is savings and investment. Let us cast our mind at the parable of the talents from the New Testament, which is necessary for us to understand the relevance of savings and investment. The wealthy man who was embarking on a journey distributed some cash to his servants based on their abilities. So he was meticulous while considering how many talents (currency) he would give to each person. Every other servant invested the money which in return yielded profits according to the value of the capital, except the lazy and irrational one he gave only one talent. He couldn't think outside the box that even if he was afraid to trade with the money, he would have saved the money in the bank and made gains from the interest.

WEALTH ACQUIRED THROUGH CONNECTION
The secret of many a man's success in the world resides in his insight into the moods of men and his tact in dealing with

them - J. G. Holland

Every business empire must come in contact with people, ranging from the relationship that exists between employers and employees at one hand, and at other hand we see more interactions extended to the customers or clients. The kind of workforce a business venture has also determines its success. To acquire wealth through connection or networking means that it is derived from coming into contact with the right people at the right time. Every successful business is built on a strong partnership with customers to ensure the elongation of its life span.

One of the ways you can tell a tree is by its fruit. People become what they are because of the life style they choose to live, and most importantly, the kind of friends or people they associate with. A manager surrounds himself with the kind of people that reflects and reinforces his business culture. By developing a business culture, the manager sets priorities in terms of the structure of Business Empire he wants to build. He also adjusts his behaviour so that he can reach his goals. There are two kinds of people in your life: those that add and multiply your riches and those that subtracts and divide your riches. From the time the struggle begins to the time you wish to erect a magnificent business empire, you must have come in contact with people who assisted you in one way or the other. It suffices that there no recluse in the art of wealth creation. Let me give a historical example. Because Spain did not exist as one united nation, their involvement in the acquisition of overseas wealth was a delayed one. The 1469 marriage between Ferdinand who in 1479 became the king of Aragon and Isabella who had earlier became the Queen of Castile five years after their marriage was a decisive connection which paved way for the greatness of Spain. The effect of that contact and the consequent marriage was that the two cities, Aragon and Castile became one formidable nation known today as Spain.

Keeping the right friends does not however mean that one should depend on them for riches. You must strike a balance (strategic alliance). What it means is that the benefit should not be tilted to one side. Living parasitic lifestyle is a bad omen in your contact circle. If you are the one initiating the contact try and find out what the interests of your partner are, and the areas he will likely benefit from you. Queen Isabella had interest in religion. Christopher Columbus could use his religious fervour to arouse the Queen's interest to endorse his exploration westward. He had convinced the Queen that it would be possible to conquer the east for Christianity by sailing westward. He also promised to promote the power and glory of Spain. It is evident that acquiring wealth through connection or partnership depends on certain exchange. Columbus used his labour for his own economic benefit. He also conferred some benefits to the Queen and the Spanish society in exchange of his interest in exploration. What followed was that in 1492 Queen Isabella granted Columbus a royal chatter giving him one-tenth of all profits for his labour.

The significance of the narrative is that you cannot give out what you don't have. Conversely, what you have determines what you get. If for instance you are searching for a juicy job, you must also possess the skillset required of such job. In that sense you are exchanging your capability for wealth. Again, young minds should make it a point of duty to develop different business contacts beyond their present circle. Columbus was an ambitious explorer. In this age we would refer to him as an entrepreneur. He extended his contact to Spain when King John II of Portugal turned down his offer to sail to some islands in Asia. He had believed, though erroneously that the route to the wealth of the East lay westward. It could be said that the maps he used were delusional. But his voyages gave Spain leadership in the discovery and colonization of the New World. You can see that the contact wasn't parasitical; each party had something to benefit. Another lesson to learn here is that you shouldn't work on your dreams based on the success of others. Understanding oneself helps in building relationships with others. Entrepreneurs are known for doing something new that will challenge them to grow. They form new relationships that will make them grow mentally, spiritually and financially. If you surround yourself with great friends and ideas, people will be confident enough to do business with you because they have more reason to trust you. And anyone who wants to find you trouble will give it a second thought.

In the final analysis, the best connection is found in the spiritual realm. The conversation between us and our spirit world reasoning is the ultimate route to wealth.

CHAPTER FIVE

HABITS OF WEALTH MANAGERS

We are what we repeatedly do. Excellence, then, is not an act but a habit- Aristotle

There is another thing that is germane for us to bear in mind when we want to prosper: That's the habit of wealth managers. Habit is what you consistently do, that at the end it becomes part of your lifestyle. In this passage we are going to learn the secrets behind the success stories of wealthy men which they have practiced over the time before they achieved something worthwhile in life. They have continued to hold steadfast unto the practices. Let me tell you something. The fact that you are working or doing business, and money flows into your account doesn't guarantee your way to financial dominion. That work or business would not necessarily build you the kind of house you desire. It may not buy you the car of your choice. I have seen people who earn good money yet they beg others or exhaust their income as soon as it gets to their bank account. Until you imbibe the right habits in your pursuit of happiness, you may not understand the true meaning of becoming wealthy.

In the preceding chapter I discussed how men acquire wealth. Now, let us discuss those codes that sustain wealth.

Save and Invest

It is the act of being financially disciplined. Keynesian economics sees it as the amount of money left over after meeting other cost and personal expenses. I have noticed from my enquiries that entrepreneurship and savings are not mutually exclusive but they are mutually reinforcing. You cannot separate the two variables and you hardly have one without the complementary role of the other. Put differently, your tactfulness as an entrepreneur will yield positive results provided you are saving and reinvesting. The ability to discipline oneself and save much money as possible is a very rewarding habit successful entrepreneurs have cultivated over the years. I realized the power of savings at a very early stage in life. In those days, and it's still a practice today, people would make up for themselves a saving box with a tiny opening where the money slips inside. Once you think you have saved enough inside the box, the safe will be broken, and by then you would have saved enough money to buy whatever you need or engage in any business it can fund.

The importance of savings as a rewarding habit cannot be overemphasized. Savings as well as investments are like taking good care of soldiers so that they may be useful to the states during the time of war. We saw how Joseph in the Bible stored up corns in great abundance in the land of Egypt during the seven years of plenty. His ability to interpret dreams with exactitude endeared him close to King Pharaoh. He magnificently rose to eminence as it pleased the king. In fact, the grain Joseph stored or saved was compared to the sand of the sea that it became difficult to be measured. So when the famine he attributed to Pharaoh's dream came upon the land of Egypt, there was enough bread to feed the people both far and beyond.

It's evident from the story that work comes before savings. You will save nothing if you don't work out something. The book of proverbs 10:5 aptly says: " He that gathereth in summer is a wise son: but he that sleepeth in harvest is a son that causeth shame". Successful managers do not cause shame rather they are the pride of the society because they have imbibed the act of savings to prosper.

I had a whimsical experience with my father when I was growing up. I was only twelve. One day he asked me to get my passport photographs ready, that we will need it for something the next day. What could that be? He kept me in suspense until the time we walked into the bank where he opened a savings account for me. The lesson was enormous. Saving money at that stage made it easier for me to accomplish specific goals. Saving money is a reliable path to becoming financial independence. Though some parents open bank account for their kids at birth, in my own case I was left with the power to make decisions on how much I deposit and then make some random choice on how to spend the money. There is no doubt that when you are saving money and investing, you feel much positive about it. In spite of this, most entrepreneurs are frugal when it comes to spending. If you are getting new things or you have things that you do not necessarily need, it makes economic sense to sale them off and make more money. If you don't negotiate price when making purchases, that does not make you a lesser wealthy man. But when you negotiate effectively, you save more money which is additional accumulation.

Adapt to change

A business idea mooted in a society in which sales are done by exchanging products for money at a nodal business point or outlet is different from that in which a virtual based society brings forth. The Internet has influenced the way we do business; from the Internet banking to placing orders for goods and services on the World Wide Web and lots more, businesses have been driven to the next level. It's therefore in the habit of a good entrepreneur to adapt to changes when it's necessary. For instance, if there were no computers, Bill Gates wouldn't have thought of inventing computer software. Man has shown his sense of inventiveness from time immemorial. Our changeover from the use of crude tools to more sophisticated equipment testify to human progress in the area of displaying greater skills to create quality goods and services in the society. Bill Gates exploited the opportunities computers afford to build software which makes its operations easier, faster and efficient.

Nevertheless, a smart entrepreneur studies the situation well before he invents or invests. It doesn't mean that he is scared of taking risks. He never takes a worthless risk. Henry Ford in his writing prefers being shown how a new idea works than to rush into it. He sees scepticism or the act of cautiousness as the balance wheel of civilization. I think Ford is right. When you are thinking of investing your hard earned money, take your time to find out every detail about the business before you embark on the investment. Never see a business opportunity that passed you by as a waste. More opportunities are on the way. The truth of the matter is that any financial decision made in a hurry has the tendency of crashing half way. Make sure you understand everything relating to the investment properly to avoid poor financial decisions.

Be inquisitive

Develop the habit of getting as much information as possible in relation to everything involved in your business and financial decisions. Wealthy men are always inquisitive. Information is a powerful tool they deploy in making exploits in business world. There can be no better way one can know where the secret of wealth lies if not through the information at one's disposal. To become successful in your chosen field or area of practice, you need to have the right information that will facilitate your breakthrough. Successful wealth managers are always in the business of managing and sharing information. They want to access information, to know what is happening around them and to develop new ideas. What they do at this point is to discard any information that won't transform their business and focus on important ones. Let me give an example. In typical oil producing Nigerian society where scarcity of petroleum products was a recurring decimal in the 1990s, you could see people scathing every nook and crannies for gas stations that sell those products. I witnessed it while growing up in Nigeria. Most times, you would find out that the reason there was no queues in gas stations amidst scarcity is because people never knew that it was dispensing- due mainly to lack of information. In business sphere, information enables us to discover areas solutions need to be provided. Information is more of the life-wire of every successful business.

The question you need to answer is whether there is hope in the path you have queued up, or would you rather seek for more information to move into a favourable environment where you can fetch as much as you can in this stream of life. The substance of the information in one's disposal places him on a better footing to understand the business environment. This explains why successful men don't joke with any form of information. In our age, information is digitalized. We need more effort in this regard. For instance, it has often been said that if the leaders of the Allied forces during the World War II had read Mien Kamft, a book revealing Adolf Hitler's intentions and struggles, they would have been armed with essential information on how best to deal with him. Inquisitiveness therefore entails pushing beyond one's present understanding.

Be time conscious

Time is the best thing one needs to invest in one's business. It must be well planned and managed. In other words, every minute must count. If you would not be able to handle a business transaction by yourself, give whoever will undertake the business on your behalf deadline behind the real time you need the deal to be completed. Wealth managers use diaries to assign tasks to themselves. They also take note of the dates and time the tasks will be accomplished according to priority.

Let me go on a personal reminiscence. In 2013, as a young entrepreneur, I got a contract to print advert flyers for an indigenous plastic company in Nigeria. Then, with a quick mental leap, the gallons and drums I saw in the factory were enough for me to develop the content of the flyer in my own imagination. And it was really fantastic. "You have two days to produce these flyers, after which we will pay you", the stout looking Lebanese manager of the company instructed me. "Sir, the design will be ready this evening, but I will need your email to forward it for your perusal and approval" I retorted with a deep enthusiasm that I was not going to fail. I had hoped to deliver the job timely as we agreed.

The email address, instead of an advance payment was the only thing I collected for the job, and swiftly left for my office, because he insisted he would not pay until the job is delivered. He had a legitimate reason - the company never knew my office address but liked my composure, and decided to give my chance of doing business with them a trial. Within some few hours the manager endorsed the graphic sample of the flier I sent to his email and asked me to go ahead with the job. It now behoved on my printer to deliver the job tome. After two days, I was yet to hear from the printer, and he was nowhere to be found. By that time the cymbal sound of my phone had become imminent from telephone calls steadily put across by the administrative unit. The lady whose voice I heard on the phone spoke with contempt. She explained how furiously the manager expressed that our business was about to flop. She was the same woman who had convinced the manager that she knew me to be a very trustworthy person even when she never met me until the day I visited the factory for the first time. So when my printer finally surfaced with the flyers, I paid him off and went to deliver the printed materials to my new client. On my arrival, I met the manager well relaxed. Even though I could not see disgust on his face, no amount of plead could stem the torrents of his anger about how untimely the flyers got to the factory. The only thing he said to rescind the price he agreed to pay me for the project was that he will deduct five per- cent of the total charge, maybe to compensate himself for the inconveniences my late arrival caused him. I agreed, hoping to safeguard future contracts - but that was not to be.

To cut the story short, I was not time conscious. Though I won the contract, I did not make the terms in the agreement. And whether it was my own making or the fault of my printer is inconsequential. What looks like a small mistake has messed up the contract.

But this very mistake made it well suitable for me to address timeliness as a good habit of an entrepreneur.

Hold steadfast

Imagine being at the edge of having financial breakthrough in your business and all of a sudden you watch your business fall like a ninepin for reasons you can't explain. Do you quit or start afresh? Real entrepreneurs do not quit. It is called perseverance. But it's financially wise to have life insurance to cover your family and all their needs in case of any eventuality. Enough of this digression! Now, do not rely on perseverance without keeping a well thought plan afloat. Perseverance becomes a key code when you are diligently working on your plans without giving up. All you need to do is to believe in yourself and keep your dreams alive. There are lessons to learn from few entrepreneurs who would have easily allowed their dreams to ooze away if they had lacked self-confidence.

Drawing from a modern example will be useful for us to understand the power of perseverance. In 1995 J. K. Rowling wrote her first Harry Potter book. Then, about twelve different publishing houses refused to accept the book as a quality work, and it was rejected. Sad and devastated, we may conclude if we dare read her mind. However, during that period, she was facing daunting life challenges ranging from a divorce to economic hardship. So when Bloomsbury, a small publisher at that time finally decided to purchase the book, she was told that she had no promising future in writing. The advice was that she should pick up a paid job. Rowling, understanding the limitations on her writing ability wholeheartedly believed in herself. What she did was not to give up; rather she learnt from her experience during her first outing as an author, buckled up and stormed the centre stage with her subsequent books. Today, in what seems to be a twist of fate, J. K. Rowling, through her Harry Potter books is one of the richest entertainers in the world. From her story, we learnt that hard work and dedication can pay off even when your chance of making it big is in doubt.

The hypothetical question about waking up one morning to find out that your business has slipped into comatose explains that life comes with its vicissitudes. So when the tide turns against you, do not give up. If you patiently remain focused while working hard according to the dictates of the time, you will prosper again because there is never a last chance to prosper in life.

Create your own business philosophy

Establish guiding principles that would spell out what your business stands for, or how it operates. For example, the business philosophy of your enterprise could be that you don't invest in an unfamiliar business. The practice is to focus on the business that will not pose a herculean task to navigate through. The embodiment of this rule in our time is Nigerian born business man, Aliko Dangote who ranks as one of the richest men in Africa. Dangote had once regretted investing in business he couldn't control. For him, any business the top managers cannot wake up in the night and explain the nitty-gritty of the business from A to Z amounts to an exercise in futility. Dangote group was into banking industry, but it was dropped or closed up because they failed to understand the process since they were not professional bankers. It is evidently clear that when you have predilections for a business you understand better, prosperity is mostly guaranteed. In 2017, Dangote group faced the worse challenge in Nigeria as a result of fall in oil price. The plummeting price caused the oil to be sold for 30 USD per barrel against its initial price of 120 USD, and then the currency was devaluated to cushion the effect. How did they survive it? For them to retain their profitability, they cut the cost of production. In other words, instead of incurring loss in the business, the profit was maintained if not doubled. So it pays to invest in business you understand pretty well. In America, J.P. Morgan was versed in financial enterprise. Carnegie pitched with Steel industry he understood better, and Rockefeller was respected in oil sector.

Mentorship

It is expedient to choose business mentor wisely. He must be someone who has business clout or you pay the price of choosing a wrong mentor. His decisions may not always be rational, so be wary. But learn from his experience because it is very important for the future of your business. Don't ever get tired of asking him important questions. Demonstrate to him that you are enterprising and ready to learn. By this he will not see his effort in futility. He will dedicate more time to reel out the truth, protect your interest and finance you if need be.

Steve Jobs was Mark Zuckerberg's mentor and he credits part of his success story at Facebook to Steve's inspiring mentorship. There is this kind of authority mentors carry with them. Whatever they say can be applied in different situations. You hardly find it difficult to situate their advice in your consciousness due to the kind of power they wield. There must not be an immediate interface between you and the mentor you admire. The most important thing is to find out from the people you are looking up to is their views on who is who, what is what and how best it is done in the enterprise. You can also learn how best to climb on the shoulders of successful men through their works or what is written about them. Always have an eye on many successful businesses. But don't fail to mind your own business. It helps to build your development firmly.

CHAPTER SIX
HUMAN RESPONSE TO GREATNESS

You are never too old to set another goal or to dream a new dream- C.S. Lewis

There are signs that we have come to full load. The number of unemployed graduates in developing countries has perpetually increased. Government institutions cannot absorb all the job seekers. Following the downturn in economic growth, job insecurity hit the headlines in 2015 as some private sectors in Nigeria laid off their employees on the account that they had no sufficient fund to pay their workers' salaries. Some state governments reportedly owed their civil servants. And there is fear that there will be many more such events if the oil price continues to plummet in the global market.

I feel that with visionary political leadership, developing countries can provide the desired job security by embracing diversification. Diversification helps to reduce the risks from engaging in too few businesses by involving in many others. Wealth manager diversifies by adding more strips to the bow (spreading investment). Although governments can diversify the economy in areas they have comparative advantage, this is not the case for small businesses. The entrepreneur focuses on providing, and or performing activities in unique ways that create more value in a competitive market. This is known as competitive advantage. He gains a competitive advantage by increasing the value of their products and services than other competitors in the market. Therefore, the superiority or quality of the value of your production above other competitors is what gives you the utmost advantage. You become a business champion either by being affordable with superior goods and services or by being unique and command customers' respects better than other competitors.

However, there is hope for staggering nations if the citizens can provide job security by creating more jobs. Though it is impractical for any nation to achieve full employment, this book argues that entrepreneurs can cooperate with governments to provide public goods as well as private goods for efficient functioning of the society. It makes economic sense for governments to maintain a structural unemployment level. It favours the government because when there are shakeups or changes in demand for labour in all facets of the economy it makes human capital to swing freely, become cheap and affordable to the government. In other words, no society can sufficiently rely on the government to provide job for all her citizens. The United States former president, John F. Kennedy during his famous inaugural speech said:

My fellow Americans ask not what your country can do for you; ask what you can do for your country.

Entrepreneurship should rise and rise in the world. We have to regard it as what societies need to see poverty off. Our generation has mostly confined themselves to the old tradition of using money, in lieu of ideas, to create wealth. But the truth is that the market economy has become very saturated. The saturation of the market economy ultimately translates to high-tech competition. What is in vogue now is knowledge or information economy. Those who think differently and engage themselves in doing new things increase their wealth. The assumption that insufficient finance dwarfs or hinders the growth of businesses is not so intuitively correct. Although lack of fund is the major challenge facing most entrepreneurs, if you don't have a good business plan and you are given huge amount of money to go into business, the possibility that you will come back cup-hand begging for more money will be huge. It is therefore within the purview of wealth management to have a good business plan before chasing after funds. A business plan is a written document that fully describes a proposed business idea. It states in concrete terms, the current state of a business, the future vision for the venture, target market analysis and challenges to be dismantled, sales and marketing strategies and how to generate and manage funds to achieve stated goals. In a nutshell, a good business plan must address issues bordering on the people, opportunities, context, and the risk and reward involved in the new venture. When you have a good business plan in place it will not only help your loan application, it helps you to allocate resources properly, handle unforeseen complications and make good business decisions. Understanding these understandable differences between having a clear business vision and dependency on money for prosperity in business will be instructive for budding entrepreneurs and existing managers to always bank on their business ideas.

The tiny few in society who think and question the old ways of doing things are the ones looking at the stars. Mark Zuckerberg falls into the category of the tiny few. The tiny few are those who understand that the world has transitioned from the brawn to the brain, from belief in manual labour to belief that knowledge worker will create more and more value than any class of worker. The most significant of these changes is the one brought about by Facebook. As a product of talent which does not require physical labour, it gave the world something she really needs. Zuckerberg and his team have continued to respond to consumers' browsing behaviour by improving what they want rather than what the organization wants them to want. The idea is known as customer relationship management.

Notably, Mark was not rich before creating Facebook. Mark hinged on his talent to create wonderfully programmed software, and with time he converted it into value. He first started by developing games for college students. As a matter of fact, FaceMash which preceded Facebook was built for fun. It was a website he hosted as a sociology and computer science student at Harvard University, Illinois, where visitors to the site had to choose between two pictures the one that was looking "hotter" than the other. Surprisingly, student journalists reacted through the campus paper that he posted students pictures without their permission which was improper. This led to the closure of the site. Later on, Mark in collaboration with two of his roommates launched Facebook. The social networking website was later introduced to other campuses, and gradually the popularity spread across the globe. It was accepted by young and old because it serves as a conduit for connecting family and friends who have lost contact over a period of time.

Mr Zuckerberg did not make it just because he has talents. If you have abundant skills yet you live in adequate poverty, how else would you show others that being skilful is profitable? It is like the life of a lawyer who goes into a courtroom to speak big grammar but fails to win his case. He who understands how to transform the pinnacle of his skills to fortune will become prosperous. This is to say that someone may know how to become rich but is not able to do so. Therefore, a skilled entrepreneur should have flair for perceiving where his skills are required, and then map out far-reaching plans to achieve his goals. He must be able to understand the circumstances and the limitations of his capabilities and how best to improve on them.

Over the years, we have seen people doing the same thing and in the same way over and over again without any modification. Even when our experience has shown clearly that what worked for Judas might not necessarily work for Peter; we still adhere strictly to the practice of imitating others. If writing, for example is lucrative all of us will turn to writers overnight. If this happens, the readers will become tut-tutting judges and may likely conclude that the age of quality writing has gone extinct until there is a new trend or writing style.

This is how pathetic the condition of Third World countries has become. As an undergraduate in a Nigerian university, I had two friends who were admitted to study law and medicine respectively. Both of them wanted to become professionals but their poor academic performance constantly proved them wrong. At a point, the law student was seen professing publicly his newly developed aversion for studying law. Then, the Dean of the faculty whom he had written to transfer him to another faculty where he could utilize his academic capacity had often interfered with good intentions to make him work hard in his law courses.

The case of the medical student was even worse. He could not pass his medical school exams, and was shown the door out. I learnt he later gained a fresh admission into another university to study a different course. Though their chances of improvement were abound, it was purely a foundational problem. They were not prepared for their chosen course of study. You do not go into any business because others are doing it. Even if you managed to remain in the business, it's because you now understand the process. It is true that poor business choices can bring pain to us, but we can grow through it and not in it. It is either the pain subdues you or you come out like a champion. The hallmark of a champion is to devote his energy and time to the cause he champions. He does not believe that constant failures are the end of his dreams.

Sequel to the brief case studies I cited above, I think the greatest need of our generation is to treat independent of thought based on feasible action plans and devotion as eleventh commandment. Any effort made to avoid sterile bandwagon will be our best bet. Imitation comes in different folds; the worst of it is to blindly follow a practice that has not proved to make you a better manager.

Getting to Start-up

Something gives my generation a profound concern. They decry the amount of wealth rich men have garnered in our time. The fear is that wealthy men have taken a considerable amount of available resources, and therefore what is left is only a chunk of it. But to allay your fears, I must tell you that the amount of wealth they have made is but a small part of what is yet to be tapped. If you can manage thousands of money you can equally manage millions of money. Efficient management of resources is the gateway to big businesses.

This book does not instruct you to kill or steal to make wealth, but early in the morning you must wake up with new entrepreneurial ideas. The most essential part of the idea is to create wealth legitimately. We are to remember that the first qualification of an entrepreneur is the dependency on his ideas to solve problems and provide the societal needs which mostly have economic rewards. For example, where people find it difficult to buy bread or eat the bread of their choice, an entrepreneur will intervene by providing the nicest bread. If an entrepreneur gets himself acquainted with the realities in his environment, it makes it easy for him to understand what the society needs. When he obtains this first-hand information, he will now have a better understanding of how to fine-tune his ideas to match the prevailing circumstances or the realities on ground. We also depend on his ideas to confer certain benefits to us as much as we patronize his products and services.

As I would always say, there is no sky rocket science involved in this process. Young minds desirous to be the next Bill Gates or Mark Zuckerberg should stop searching for demons to cast out. We are always tempted to link any bad lot in our lives to spiritual machinations, and heap all the blames for being poor on demons. I do not doubt the existence of spiritual machinations. From my little knowledge of the Bible, I have not only read where demons were casted out but I also understand that the things that happen in the physical have first occurred in the spiritual realm before manifestation. You can believe it and you can also pray over it. But our spirituality should influence us to believe in our capacity to invoke our talents and skills to tackle whatever spiritual challenge that has manifested in the physical. Things will only get better when you believe and take charge of your destiny. The fear to try something new is the greatest demon that lives in us. Instead of chasing shadows, we must focus attention on our talents. Talents are important but your attitude towards your talent is more important.

A few cases will elucidate the points I made above. During the middle ages, Iberian Peninsula was situated in a nodal point that has been described as the south west street corner of Europe. This made it so difficult for economic exploitation. What did the European conquistadors do? They simply seized the opportunity the challenge of the position posed to them to improve their caravel and penetrate into the Iberian territory for occupation. In another scenario, if it was not for the trust Soichiro Honda had in his skills without any formal education when he was turned down for an engineering job by Toyota, he wouldn't have founded Honda automobiles. He didn't blame his rejection on any demon. It was really a blessing in disguise, because he utilized his technical expertise to introduce a new brand into automobile industry.

Now, let us discuss what should rather worry my generation. I have argued in the first chapter that wealth does not create people, people create it. When we talk so much about capital, what comes to our mind is man- made instrument of production that has been designed to accelerate further productions. Capital can be defined as assets capable of generating resources for the business. Or put differently, it is a means of production that has already been produced. It comprises cash, inventory and fixed assets. There are three (3) types of capital an entrepreneur needs to get himself acquainted with before starting up a business, namely working capital, fixed capital and human capital

Working capital
According to Business Dictionary, working capital is the cash available for day-to –day operations of an organization. Working capital is needed in servicing the business. When you minus current liabilities from the current assets of your business, you will get the working capital which now tells you how efficient you operate the business and also the company's short term financial health. If the ratio is less than 1 it means a negative working capital and can lead to bankruptcy. At the other hand, a high working capital means that you have excess inventory or cash that's not invested.

Fixed capital
These are tangible assets needed for business operations, such as tools, machinery and facilities. It does not however mean that the items are stationed at one place. Though factories, offices or shops are not movable, the term fixed is coined because money spent on those durable goods is fixed or unrealized for a long period, in contrast with working capital that can be realized as soon as goods made with them are sold. These assets are also considered fixed because they are not consumed or destroyed during production of goods and services, but can be used and used over again.

Human capital
Human capital is defined as the collective skills, knowledge or other intangible assets possessed by individuals that can use to create economic values. This is where the roles of the entrepreneur become pronounced. An entrepreneur is the greatest asset to any business venture. He transforms his skillset into economic value. The more we invest in human capital, the more the labour will be-

come qualitative. Human capital generates material wealth for businesses. The success of any business or organization is dependent on how human capital is organized.

I want to propose that those who are able to understand the challenges in starting up a new business without cash should be made to understand advantageous ways of starting with a limited fund. I understand the financial challenges facing hordes of entrepreneurs. During the times of Julius Caesar, he distributed land to the poor. There was also law of bankruptcy that helped people who could not pay their debts. Not only that such law may not exist in our own time, I would submit laconically that new businesses, especially small ones should avoid obtaining loans for start-up. Loan payments make new small business vulnerable to high interest rates, except in cases where the manager uses his good character as collateral. In other words, in terms of making regular loan, the possibility of having irregular cash flow should bother the entrepreneur. A good manager should crosscheck if revenues from his business can cover the relevant cost of production, services or purchases. He also needs to consider the lending interest rate. It is now the outcome of these calculations that determines if loan is a considerable option.

Given the challenges facing budding managers to raise money for their ventures, the options for them will range from partnering with people who share the same idea or becoming an affiliate marketer to outsourcing the services or products, and to seek for credit facilities from philanthropists, government and nongovernmental organizations. Some service oriented businesses are not capital intensive- leveraging the power of internet opens many windows for prosperity. If you are desirous of becoming an entrepreneur you should not give up on your dreams simply because you do not have the start-up fund required in the business. The sweetest money to spend is the one acquired through one's exceptional skills. In that same manner, these days or in our time, Angels enjoy expending their energy to support skilled entrepreneurs. If you are talented or skilled in a specific niche, you already have the resource with which you can command support. The role that particularly belongs to those who wish to become wealth managers is picking up responsibilities that suit their ability.

Nevertheless, there is no better way we can overcome poverty if not by creating sustainable wealth. The idea of sustainability in wealth creation is to ensure that it meets the needs of the present society as well as the needs of next generations. Nelson Mandela, the first black president of South Africa, saw the battle against poverty as an idea of justice, and for Plato, justice is the good life of the whole. Thus, justice can only be justifiable when a good number of people including men and women in the street who have not had it so good are all happy. The future lies on us. The world is still in need of the generosity of mankind; those who are eager to live a fulfilled life should be ambitious and kind enough to invest in our society without compromising the ability of the future generation to achieve the will of their age.

In the nearest decades, digital entrepreneurs would likely champion a new revolution- an entre-revolution that would bring new club of men to positions of economic power. The moment our generation starts acting as the allegorical lion and antelope, we won't be far from effecting the desired change in the world.

In Africa, every morning an Impala (antelope) wakes up knowing that it must outrun the fastest lion if it desires to stay alive (to become wealthy). Again, every morning a lion wakes up knowing that it must outrun the slowest Impala or it will starve (to become poor). It makes no difference of you are impala or lion, when the sun comes up in Africa, you must wake up running (mental and physical labour)

- Zambian Literature (the emphases in parenthesis are mine)

It doesn't really make any difference if you are rich or poor now. You must hit the ground running with great ideas. In African mythology, the old woman who said that she would not run was forced to run when the goat took her tobacco container, but then it was too late. Now is still early. Tomorrow may never come. The time to start chasing the tobacco container is now.

REFERENCES

Adams Smith (1776) an Enquiry into the Nature and Causes of the Wealth of the Nation, W. Straham and T. Cadell, London

Bob Nelson and Peter Economy (2005) The Management Bible, John Wiley & Sons Inc.

Iwelegbu A.I, Okafor A.N. (2003) the History of Economic Thought, Akajon Publishers, Awka, Nigeria

John B. Cark, A.M. (1894) Philosophy of Wealth, Ginn & Company, Publishers Boston, U.S.A pg. 2-9

John Law (1705) Money and Trade Considered, the Heirs and Successors of Andrew Anderson

Kelvin Shillignton (2012) History of Africa-Third Edition, Palgrave Macmillan pg.167

Nnamdi Azikiwe (1971) My Odyssey, Hurst & Co

Lee Kuan Yew (2000) From Third World to First, New York, Harper Collins

German Arciniegas (2003) Caribbean Sea of the New World, Markus Wiener publishers

Henry Ford (2003) My Life and Work, 1st World Library Society, Fairfield

Jefferson Steve "When Raising Funds, Start-Ups Face the Debt vs. Equity Question" pacific Business news, 3 August 2001

Daniel Roselle (1963) A World History, Ginn Books pg.121-125

Dess Gregory G., G.T. Lumkin and Alan B. Eisner, Strategic Management: Text and Cases, Boston: McGraw-Hill Irwin, 2006

John S. Gordon, an Empire of Wealth: Epic History of American Economic Power, Harper Collins

Tim Hindle (2008) Guide to Management Ideas and Gurus, Profile Books Ltd.

Thomas Piketty (2013), Capital in the 21st Century, Harvard University Press.

J.H Parry (1963) the Age of Reconnaissance, University of California Press

Walter Rodney, (1972) How Europe Underdeveloped Africa, Bogle-L'Ouverture Publications, UK

Office of Small Business Development Centres, US Small Business Administration, Available from http//www.sba.gov/sbdc/aboutus.html

Eric Beinhocker, The Origin of Wealth: Evolution, Complexity and the Radical Remaking of Economics, Harvard Business Review Press. 2007 pg. 261-262

www.economydetail.blogspot.com.ng

www.schalkenbach.org/library/henry-george/science-of-political-economy/spe203.html

www.un.org >2016/08

www.computerworld.com/artice/3052218/the-massive-panama-papers-data-leak-explained.amp.html

www.britannica.com/topic/Standard-Oil

www.crf-usa.org/bill-of-rights-in-action/bria-19-2-b-social-darwinism-laissez-faire-capitalism.html

www.braitannica.com/topic/Facebook

www.forbes.com/lists/2011/89/africa-billionaires-11_land.html

www.alibabagroup.com/en/about/history

https://en.wikipedia.org/wiki/Arap_Spring

https://www.youtube.com/watch?v=OBnQ21NSpMw

https://en.wikipedia.org/wiki/List_of_wealthiest_historical_figures

https://www.investopedia.com/terms/s/savings.asp

https://www.theguardian.com/world/2015/mar/20/students-attack-cecil-john-rhodes-statue-south-africa-university-cape-down-questions-race

https://www.dailymail.co.uk/news/article-5605071/What-FaceMash-Zuckerberg-grilled-Congress-Facebook-origins.html

https://www.entrepreneur.com/article/316782

www.ingramcontent.com/pod-product-compliance
Lightning Source LLC
Chambersburg PA
CBHW080629220526
45467CB00011B/3425